S0-APX-933

BRENT'S BOT

By Tessa Greene
Illustrated by Bojana Stojanovic

Cover design by Robin Fight

© 2021 Jenny Phillips

goodandbeautiful.com

CHALLENGE WORDS:

idea

robot

wheels

when

worked

Brent looked out. It was wet, and he felt sad.

"What is the matter,
Brent?" asked Mom.

"I feel sad that I have no one to play with," said Brent.

4

"Yes, that can feel sad," Mom said.

"Can you think of a
way to have fun?"

"I think so," Brent said. "Do you think I can?"

"I think you can!"
said Mom.

She gave Brent
a big hug.

Brent went to his room.

Brent spotted a big ball...

...but playing ball
takes two kids.

Brent saw puppets...

...but there was no one to see him.

Then Brent saw a
book with a robot.

Brent had a big idea.

Brent worked hard on
his big idea all day.

He worked the next day.
He worked for three days!

Brent used lots of old cans.
Brent used some tools.

He used the wheels from
his old wagon.

Then Brent's big
idea was done!

Brent put a sheet on his big idea, so Mom did not see it yet.

Brent told his big idea to Mom.

"May I see what you have worked on?" asked Mom.

"Yes!" said Brent. Brent
smiled big and took
the sheet off.

"Ta-da!" Brent yelled. Under the sheet was a robot!

"Wow!" said Mom. "What is this?"

"This is Bot!" said Brent.

"He will play with me,
so I am not sad!"

"Wow! Good job,
Brent," said Mom.

"Bot is very neat! What
will you do first?"

"I think we will play ball," said Brent.
"What do you think, Bot?"

Bot made a sound: "Beep-boop!"

"That means yes!" said Brent.
"Come on, Bot!"

Brent took Bot to
the backyard.

"This is a good spot
to play ball," he said.

"Beep-boop-beep!" said Bot.
Bot rolled back on his wheels.

"Oh," said Brent, "does that mean
you do not know how to play ball?"

"Beep-boop," said Bot.

That means yes.

"That is OK. I will teach you," Brent said. "It's easy!"

Brent tossed the ball to Bot. "Now you toss it back," he told Bot.

Bot's arms went up and down.
The ball did not go very far.

Bot rolled back on
his wheels again.

"Do not fear, Bot; you will see!" Brent said.

Brent and
Bot tossed
the ball
back and
forth.

Bot got good at tossing
the ball to Brent!

"Good job, Bot!" said
Brent. "You are good
at playing ball."

"What do we do next?"

Brent and Bot went to Brent's room to find a game to play.

Brent saw his puppets.

"Bot, should we have a
puppet play?" Brent asked.

45

"Beep-boop!" Bot said.

That means yes!

Brent took out his puppets.

"You sit here, and I will put on a play," Brent told Bot.

Bot liked Brent's play!

The play
ended, and
Bot came to
Brent.

"Boop-beep-beep!"
Bot said.

"Does that mean you want
a turn?" asked Brent.

"Beep-boop," Bot said. He hoped to do the next play.

"I'm not done yet," said Brent.

Bot rolled back on his wheels again.

Brent had liked putting
on the play...

...but he wanted Bot
to have fun, too!

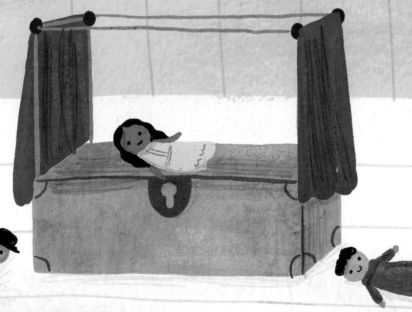

"OK, Bot," said Brent. "I had a turn,
so now you can have a turn."

When Brent and Bot
were done playing,
they ate dinner with
Mom and Dad.

"I'm glad you had so much fun playing with Bot today!" said Mom.

"Bot is a good robot!"

Brent was so happy!

When it was time for bed, Brent set
Bot at the end of his bed.

He went to sleep thinking of all the
fun they were going to have the
next day.

Check out these other Level 1B books from The Good and the Beautiful!

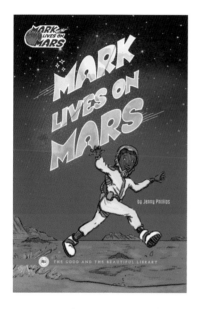

Mark Lives on Mars
By Jenny Phillips

Monkey Mayhem
By Amy Drorbaugh

goodandbeautiful.com

2.1WE401 Printed in S. Korea Mar-2024